D0139982

FIFTY YEARS OF
ATTACHMENT THEORY

THE DONALD WINNICOTT MEMORIAL LECTURE

FIFTY YEARS OF ATTACHMENT THEORY

Given by

Sir Richard Bowlby Bt

RECOLLECTIONS OF

DONALD WINNICOTT

AND JOHN BOWLBY

Given by

Pearl King

Published by
KARNAC
on behalf of
THE WINNICOTT CLINIC OF PSYCHOTHERAPY
Registered Charity No. 260427
London, 2004

Published in 2004 by
Karnac (Books) Ltd.
6 Pembroke Buildings, London NW10 6RE
on behalf of
The Winnicott Clinic of Psychotherapy
PO Box 233
Ruislip
Middlesex HA4 8UJ

Copyright © 2004 Winnicott Clinic of Psychotherapy

Foreword copyright © 2004 Eric Koops
Introduction "John Bowlby and Donald Winnicott: collegial comrades in child mental health" copyright © 2004 Brett Kahr
"Fifty years of Attachment Theory" copyright © 2004 Sir John Bowlby
"Recollections of Donald Winnicott and John Bowlby" copyright © 2004 Pearl King

The rights of the contributors to be identified as the authors of this work have been asserted with §§77 and 78 of the Copyright Design and Patents Act 1988.

All rights reserved. No part of this publication may be reproduced, stored in a retrieval system, or transmitted, in any form or by any means, electronic, mechanical, photocopying, recording, or otherwise, without the prior written permission of the publisher.

British Library Cataloguing in Publication Data

A C.I.P. for this book is available from the British Library

ISBN 1 85575 385 5

Edited, designed, and produced by The Studio Publishing Services Ltd, Exeter EX4 8JN

Printed in Great Britain

www.karnacbooks.com

CONTENTS

CONTRIBUTORS

Sir Richard Bowlby, Bt. Richard Bowlby qualified in medical and scientific photography in 1968 and, until he formally retired in 1999, had a successful career illustrating medical research; in particular, he helped to communicate the findings of the researchers with whom he worked by producing photographs and academic video-tapes. Since retiring, his main preoccupation has been to study and disseminate more widely the work of his father, Dr John Bowlby, the "begetter" of the body of knowledge which came to be known as "Attachment Theory". This argued that the ties formed between child and parents (particularly the mother), from the child's first months and throughout the early years, crucially affect personality development, particularly traits relating to self-confidence. To this end, Sir Richard maintains contact internationally with workers and organizations engaged in the field of child development and has produced training videos on Attachment Theory for profes-sionals. He lectures widely on the critical importance of early attachments (sometimes referred to as "bonding") and has become involved with innovative, community-based projects designed to help young parents and their families develop secure relationships with each other.

Brett Kahr is Senior Lecturer in Psychotherapy in the School of Psychotherapy and Counselling at Regent's College in London, as well as a psychotherapist and marital psychotherapist in private practice. In 2001, The Winnicott Clinic of Psychotherapy appointed him as the first Winnicott Clinic Senior Research Fellow in Psychotherapy. He is a Patron of The Squiggle Foundation, and a Trustee of the Institute of Psychotherapy and Disability, as well as the Special Media Adviser to The United Kingdom Council for Psychotherapy, and Consultant at the Centre for Attachment-Based Psychoanalytic Psychotherapy. His books include *D. W. Winnicott: A Biographical Portrait*, which won the Gradiva Award for Biography in 1997, as well as *Forensic Psychotherapy and Psychopathology: Winnicottian Perspectives*, and *The Legacy of Winnicott: Essays on Infant and Child Mental Health*, all published by Karnac.

Pearl King. Pearl King, in addition to having been a practising psychoanalyst since the early 1950s, is a lecturer, training supervisor and historian/archivist of the profession. She worked closely with Dr Donald Winnicott and Dr John Bowlby, all three being Members of the British Psychoanalytical Society, of which Miss King became the first non-medical President. She also served as Secretary to the International Psychoanalytical Association and was awarded the Sigourney Award, the highest honour in the discipline of psychoanalysis. *The Freud–Klein Controversies* (Routledge 1992) is one of her best-known books, translated into many different languages. She is also the editor of *No Ordinary Psychoanalyst: The Exceptional Contributions of John Rickman* (Karnac 2003); work in progress includes preparing her own collected papers for publication.

Eric Koops, LVO. Eric Koops is the Chairman of the Trustees of the Winnicott Clinic of Psychotherapy, the registered charity responsible for the annual Donald Winnicott Memorial Lecture.

The Clinic was founded in 1969 to promote professional training in the principles of psychotherapy, to conduct research, and to assist in the provision of individual psychotherapy. During the 1990s, to meet changing circumstances, assistance was extended to patients in group therapy, training grants were awarded, and symposia arranged to encourage organizations to reduce workplace stress.

Since 2000, the main focus of Clinic activities has been the wider dissemination of the work and ideas of Dr Donald W. Winnicott (1896–1971), the distinguished English paediatrician, child psychiatrist and psychoanalyst, who made an outstanding contribution to the understanding of the causes of mental illness, particularly in infants and children. To this end, the Clinic established the Winnicott Clinic Senior Research Fellowship in Psychotherapy and Counselling, and the annual Donald Winnicott Memorial Lecture, designed for a wide audience of professionals and others involved with children. Lectures focus upon specific topics arising from Winnicott's life and ideas, in terms of relevance for twenty-first century living.

Foreword

Eric Koops

As Chairman of the Winnicott Clinic of Psychotherapy my task this evening is very simple: to welcome you to the second Donald Winnicott Memorial Lecture, tell you a little about Winnicott, and hand you over to Brett Kahr, who will introduce the speakers. When we booked this particular venue we did not anticipate a problem with numbers—but we had one; there were 100 more applications than could be accommodated; that alone is surely testimony to the nature of tonight's topic and those who are participating. It's marvellous to see such a wide range in age and interest represented in the audience. Thank you for being here tonight.

We are a very small charitable trust and have, in the last two or three years, focused our attention primarily on the work and ideas of Donald Winnicott. In furtherance of that objective we have two main activities: a Senior Research Fellowship—the first of which was awarded to Brett Kahr, who is going to produce the definitive biography of Donald Winnicott in, we hope, 2004–2005; the second is this Memorial Lecture. We held our first such event almost exactly a year ago; it was a remarkable evening. Giving the Lecture was Dr Joyce McDougall, who spoke on the theme: "Donald

Winnicott the Man: Reflections and Recollections", which has now been published on our behalf by Karnac Books, to whom we are most grateful. We hope this is but the first in a long series of published Winnicott Memorial Lectures, and that tonight's deliberations will be the second such publication.

May I draw your attention to our questionnaire. It is important to us as we plan further Lectures to receive feedback from our audiences; we welcome your thoughts and ideas. From talking to various people this evening I know that an opportunity to meet others working in the same fields but in different parts of the country is valued; perhaps, if you think it worthwhile, we could begin a quarterly soirée—an occasion for people to get together to discuss mutual interests; it depends on your response and comments will be appreciated. Thank you.

Introduction of Sir Richard Bowlby

Brett Kahr

John Bowlby and Donald Winnicott: collegial comrades in child mental health

Having inaugurated the annual Donald Winnicott Memorial Lecture last year with a spirited talk by the Paris-based psychoanalyst Dr Joyce McDougall, the members of the organizing committee of The Winnicott Clinic of Psychotherapy have trawled through our address books and memory banks in order to find a suitable candidate to present the second annual Lecture. One might think that we would be spoiled for choice, but we have very exacting requirements. Above all, we wanted to find a speaker who shared Dr Donald Winnicott's passionate commitment to the fields of infant mental health and child mental health, and one who, like Winnicott, had worked relentlessly to disseminate psychological knowledge to the widest possible audience. We strove to find a lecturer who thought outward, rather than inward, and one who communicated with those rare Winnicottian qualities of charm, generosity, graciousness, and warmth. We also needed to find someone who could dare to follow in the famously zesty footsteps of Joyce McDougall.

We struck gold this year. We are quite gleeful with gratitude that Sir Richard Bowlby accepted our invitation to deliver the second annual Donald Winnicott Memorial Lecture sponsored by The Winnicott Clinic of Psychotherapy. Sir Richard has never studied psychology or psychoanalysis in the formal sense. Quite simply, he did not need to, having absorbed the most important principles at home, from a most reliable source, namely, his father, the late and much missed Dr John Bowlby. Instead, Richard Bowlby has devoted his professional life to the fields of medical illustration and scientific photography, and he headed the Department of Medical Illustration at the Royal Free Hospital and Royal Free Hospital Medical School in the University of London for many years, pioneering the use of video technology in the recording and transmission of data that might otherwise lie moribund on the printed pages of a journal.

Since his retirement from hospital work, Sir Richard has used his unique background in medical illustration and video technology to educate increasingly large audiences around the world about the fundamentals of the parent–infant bond, about the importance of attachment theory, and about the development of innovative community-based projects which help young people and their families. Those who have met Sir Richard will recognize the parallels with Donald Winnicott, both men who have treated all enquiries with utter seriousness—both men who specialized in offering exquisite and unstinting support to parents and children—both men who endeavoured, with success, to bring psychology out of the ghetto.

These Winnicottian characteristics have earned Sir Richard the Chairmanship of the Trustees of the Centre for Attachment-Based Psychoanalytic Psychotherapy, one of the most progressive and vibrant clinical training organizations in Great Britain, as well as an Honorary Research Fellowship at the Attachment Unit of the Department of Psychology at University College London, in the University of London. He also delivered, among many other noted talks, the inaugural lecture at the Centre for Child Mental Health, in London.

Needless to say, Sir Richard's family history as a member of the Bowlby clan lends a certain poignancy to our proceedings, not only as the son of the distinguished clinician, researcher, and author

Dr John Bowlby, but also because of the close historical links between Bowlby and Winnicott. Sir Richard's paternal grandfather, Sir Anthony Bowlby, the eminent surgeon who attended King George V, actually taught the young Donald Winnicott during his medical studies at St Bartholomew's Hospital in London at some point between 1917 and 1920. And Sir Richard's father, Dr John Bowlby, collaborated with Dr Donald Winnicott in many different capacities throughout the 1930s, 1940s, 1950s, and 1960s. Both Donald Winnicott and John Bowlby trained together at the fledgling Institute of Psycho-Analysis in London during the early years of psychoanalytical education in Great Britain, occasionally falling foul of the Training Committee because of their progressive ideas (Training Committee Minutes, 1926–1945). In 1939, both Bowlby and Winnicott became contributors to Dr Ronald Gordon's (1939) landmark edited text *A Survey of Child Psychiatry*, the very first British book that used the words "child psychiatry" in its title, thus giving shape to this new field of clinical endeavour. Also in 1939, John Bowlby and Donald Winnicott joined forces with the child psychiatrist Dr Emanuel Miller to co-author an important letter of deep concern to the *British Medical Journal*, warning fellow Britons about the potentially deleterious psychological sequelae of evacuating children to the countryside, and of the damaging consequences of separating children from their parents (Bowlby *et al.*, 1939). Both men also served as commentators upon the later infamous "blood-tie" case involving child maltreatment (Bowlby, 1966a; Winnicott, 1966).

The links between Bowlby and Winnicott extend even further. As the middle years of the twentieth century unfolded, both Bowlby and Winnicott assisted one another in professional contexts, by reviewing one another's work in professional periodicals, or by commenting upon one another's work at scientific meetings (e.g. Winnicott, 1953). Bowlby (1958) would personally invite Winnicott to teach clinical seminars for the child psychotherapy trainees at the Tavistock Clinic, in its old premises at 2 Beaumont Street in Central London, and Winnicott (1959) would from time to time write to Bowlby requesting a copy of some new article. When Winnicott became aggrieved that a journalist had misrepresented him in a national broadsheet, Bowlby (1966b) wrote to commiserate. And the pair turned to one another for scientific encouragement. In 1961, Bowlby wrote to Winnicott enquiring:

> In one of your papers I seem to remember you describe a girl who
> had suffered from enuresis following the death of a close relative.
> My recollection is that you made an interpretation along the lines
> that she had been very fond of the lost figure and that she then burst
> into tears and her symptom cleared up. If I am right about this I
> would be very grateful for the reference, as I would like to quote it
> in the paper on which I am now working.

The unpublished correspondence between the two men, housed
partly in the Archives of Psychiatry in the Oskar Diethelm Library at
the Institute for the History of Psychiatry, at the Joan and Sanford
I. Weill Medical College of Cornell University, in New York City,
and partly in the Pearl King Archives Trust, at the British Psycho-
analytical Society in London, reveals a warm and convivial relationship which endured over many years (cf. Winnicott, 1966). At one
point, it even seems that Bowlby had planned to collaborate with
the educational psychologist Dr Ved Varma (1970) to edit a Fest-
schrift in honour of Winnicott's seventy-fifth birthday, but alas, this
volume never materialized.

Donald Winnicott made a strong impression not only on Dr
John Bowlby, but also on Mrs Ursula Bowlby, the devoted spouse
of Dr Bowlby, and the mother of Sir Richard Bowlby. In 1957,
shortly after the publication of Winnicott's landmark book
The Child and the Family: First Relationships, based on articles and
radio broadcasts intended for a general audience, Ursula Bowlby
(1957) wrote to congratulate Winnicott:

> I just wanted to let you know how much I've enjoyed reading *The
> Child and the Family*. As you know, I had already read *The Ordinary
> Devoted Mother and her Baby* and admired it so much—indeed it has
> been the only English book which I've felt able to recommend when
> mothers have asked me for the name of a good baby-book. But that
> was some time ago and I've very much enjoyed re-reading it, and I
> find it just as recommendable and good.

Mrs Bowlby continued praising Winnicott:

> Now I am busily recommending the book to all my friends and
> relations, because it seems a tradition nowadays that every
> educated mother should read at least one baby-book, and I am all
> in favour of their reading a really good one.

With such longstanding connections between the Winnicott and Bowlby families, and because of his Bowlbian and Winnicottian qualities as a man, it gives me much satisfaction to invite Sir Richard Bowlby to present the second annual Donald Winnicott Memorial Lecture this evening on the topic "Fifty Years of Attachment Theory". Ladies and gentlemen, on behalf of The Winnicott Clinic of Psychotherapy, please join me in welcoming Sir Richard Bowlby.

Acknowledgements

I wish to extend my gratitude to Dr George Makari and Ms Diane Richardson of the Oskar Diethelm Library at the Institute of the History of Psychiatry, Joan and Sanford I. Weill Medical College at Cornell University in New York City, New York, and to Ms Pearl King at the Pearl King Archives Trust, Archives of the British Psychoanalytical Society, at the British Psychoanalytical Society, in London, for permission to utilize the Donald W. Winnicott Papers and related materials, and for their many scholarly courtesies over the years. I also want to convey my deepest appreciation to the Trustees of The Winnicott Clinic of Psychotherapy who generously appointed me as the first Winnicott Clinic Senior Research Fellow in Psychotherapy, thereby greatly facilitating my ongoing biographical research on Dr Donald Winnicott.

References

Bowlby, J. (1958). Letter to Donald W. Winnicott. 21st November. Box 1. File 8. Archives of Psychiatry. The Oskar Diethelm Library. Institute for the History of Psychiatry. Department of Psychiatry. Joan and Sanford I. Weill Medical College. Cornell University. The New York Presbyterian Hospital, New York, USA.

Bowlby, J. (1961). Letter to Donald W. Winnicott. 13th January. Box 3. File 1. Archives of Psychiatry. The Oskar Diethelm Library. Institute for the History of Psychiatry. Department of Psychiatry. Joan and Sanford I. Weill Medical College. Cornell University. The New York Presbyterian Hospital, New York, USA.

Bowlby, J. (1966a). Letter to Donald W. Winnicott. 21st March. Box 5. File 9. Archives of Psychiatry. The Oskar Diethelm Library. Institute for the History of Psychiatry. Department of Psychiatry. Joan and Sanford I. Weill Medical College. Cornell University. The New York Presbyterian Hospital, New York, USA.

Bowlby, J. (1966b). Letter to Donald W. Winnicott. 26th September. Box 6. File 1. Archives of Psychiatry. The Oskar Diethelm Library. Institute for the History of Psychiatry. Department of Psychiatry. Joan and Sanford I. Weill Medical College. Cornell University. The New York Presbyterian Hospital, New York, USA.

Bowlby, J., Miller, E., & Winnicott, D. W. (1939). Evacuation of small children. *British Medical Journal*, 16th December, 1202–1203.

Bowlby, U. (1957). Letter to Donald W. Winnicott. 8th March. Box 1. File 1. Archives of Psychiatry. The Oskar Diethelm Library. Institute for the History of Psychiatry. Department of Psychiatry. Joan and Sanford I. Weill Medical College. Cornell University. The New York Presbyterian Hospital, New York, USA.

Gordon, R. G. (Ed.). (1939). *A Survey of Child Psychiatry*. London: Humphrey Milford and Oxford University Press.

Training Committee Minutes (1926–1945). Training Ctte Minutes: 24.3.1926–29.10.1945. The Institute of Psycho-Analysis. Pearl King Archives Trust, Archives of the British Psychoanalytical Society. The British Psychoanalytical Society. London.

Varma, V. (1970). Letter to Contributors. Undated. Box 8. File 8. Archives of Psychiatry. The Oskar Diethelm Library. Institute for the History of Psychiatry. Department of Psychiatry. Joan and Sanford I. Weill Medical College. Cornell University. The New York Presbyterian Hospital. New York, USA.

Winnicott, D. W. (1953) [1989]. Discussion of "Grief and mourning in infancy". In: D. W. Winnicott (1989). *Psycho-Analytic Explorations*. C. Winnicott, R. Shepherd, & M. Davis (Eds.), pp. 426–432. London: Karnac Books.

Winnicott, D. W. (1957). *The Child and the Family: First Relationships*. London: Tavistock.

Winnicott, D. W. (1959). Letter to John Bowlby. 28th January. Box 2. File 1. Archives of Psychiatry. The Oskar Diethelm Library. Institute for the History of Psychiatry. Department of Psychiatry. Joan and Sanford I. Weill Medical College. Cornell University. The New York Presbyterian Hospital, New York, USA.

Winnicott, D. W. (1966). Letter to John Bowlby. 22nd March. Box 5. File

9. Archives of Psychiatry. The Oskar Diethelm Library. Institute for the History of Psychiatry. Department of Psychiatry. Joan and Sanford I. Weill Medical College. Cornell University. The New York Presbyterian Hospital, New York, USA.

Fifty Years of Attachment Theory

Sir Richard Bowlby

I am not a psychologist, I like to design racing cars. I lived close to my father all my life: I lived with him, in the flat above him, in the house next door to him, shared a boat on the south coast and a holiday home on the Isle of Skye. I find that I remember more about my father than I once realized. It was a psychiatrist who told me that.

It is astonishing to me, as a layman, that Attachment Theory was not greeted with a great chorus of "Hallelujah!, at last we have seen the light." It was not like that. It was a real struggle to get this concept—one of the fundamentals of what makes us human—more widely understood so that society could benefit. It is solidly based on research and, after all, what is the point of doing research if nobody knows about it? That makes it a waste of time. Even when it is obscure, as much of it can be, research data is valuable. I have spent much of my life trying to clarify research findings in medical science and assist in their wider circulation. Eventually I quit my job to communicate Attachment Theory in what I hope is a more accessible way so that it could be more broadly understood.

What I want to do tonight is to recount some of the struggles that Attachment Theory has had in gaining a wider acceptance.

It is fifty years since my father wrote *Child Care and the Growth of Love*, and although Attachment Theory is now established as a valuable working model in child development and mental health circles, the general public's knowledge of the concept of attachment is notably lacking. From my position inside the family and outside the professions, I am taking a critical look at what prevents the dissemination of the valuable insights that Attachment Theory could bring to the general public. For some years I have been presenting recollections of my father's professional struggle to develop Attachment Theory, and some of the public's misunderstandings of what he wrote. Sometimes this has been because of the emotional difficulties that they have with his work, and there are also wider social issues which still prevent many people from accepting Attachment Theory.

Probably the largest group consists of people fortunate enough to have had a secure attachment, who have the confident expectation of repeating the cycle with their own children; for this group the whole subject is so self-explanatory and obvious that it hardly merits comment—unless things go wrong.

In a way I do not even like to call it Attachment Theory any more; I prefer to call it research into bonding. For many people "theory" means a vague, "anything goes", sort of idea; it does not have only the strict scientific definition which is to be found in the dictionary.

The origin of my father's motivation for working on this conundrum of the parent–child attachment relationship probably stems from a traumatic event when he was about four years old. In 1911 his father was a successful surgeon who lived in a large London town-house with his wife and six children. The normal arrangement for child-care at that time was to have a senior nanny—she was called Nana—and one or two nursemaids who helped out as more children were born. My father was the fourth child; he had a nursemaid called Minnie who had day-to-day responsibility for him. The children rarely saw their father, except on Sundays and holidays; and they only saw their mother for an hour a day between 5.00 and 6.00 in the evening. Effectively, these children had twenty-three-hour a day good quality and non-parental care. My father grew to love Minnie, who once told his sister that John was her favourite, and my guess is that Minnie was his surrogate, principal attachment figure in preference to his own mother. Then, when he was four, Minnie left the family to get a better job. When my father spoke of this event, he said he was sufficiently hurt to feel the pain of childhood separation—but was not so traumatized that he could not face working with it on a daily basis. All this is in print; it is not a family secret.

At the age of twenty-one, my father, a disenchanted medical student, was working at Priory Gate, a school for maladjusted children (that's what they were called—people were not very "PC" in those days). Here he met John Alford, a remarkable man for whom my father had great respect and who became a professor (in Canada, I believe). Alford had noticed that many of the disturbed children in the school came from very disrupted family backgrounds. It was he who convinced my father to complete his medical degree and study psychoanalysis; he also inspired his interest in maternal deprivation, the forerunner of his later work on attachment. I imagine my father identified the loss of his Minnie with the maternal deprivation experienced by the delinquent children in the school. He undertook his study of forty-four juvenile thieves before the Second World War and it was published in 1944. He found that seventeen of the group had suffered an early prolonged, or permanent, separation from their mother, or permanent mother substitute, during the first five years of their life—as compared with only two in the control group. In order that he could be absolutely sure of the disrupted childhood these children had experienced, he recorded only death, desertion, or divorce in the families; these were the only data that he could be absolutely sure were reliable.

My father was not afraid to confront intimidating figures, which was to lead him into a series of conflicts throughout his career. It began with his protracted psychoanalytic training, when he would insist on arguing with his analyst, Joan Riviere, and his supervisor, Melanie Klein. He found it hard to accept their rigidly-held theories because he believed these failed to satisfy the scientific rigour he had learned at Cambridge when studying medicine. (I may say that Donald Winnicott was at Cambridge, too, and neither did he go much on the training; it was very rigid; there was no emotion involved; everything was very clinical.)

In 1949 the World Health Organization (WHO) invited my father to report on the psychiatric needs of the many homeless children who had been orphaned because of the Second World War. The wide-ranging material that he gathered for the WHO report, called *Maternal Care and Mental Health,* was published in 1951. The main text of the report was used for his popular and controversial paperback *Child Care and the Growth of Love,* written in 1952 and published a year later. It used to be said about him: "Stick a pin in Bowlby and out comes maternal deprivation!" At this point he was still working with the material on orphans; he had not worked out Attachment Theory. On the first page of both books he outlined the conditions needed for the healthy development of children:

> For the moment it is sufficient to say that what is believed to be essential for mental health is that the infant and young child should experience a warm, intimate and continuous relationship with his mother, or permanent mother substitute, in which both find satisfaction and enjoyment.

However, only in the paperback does he clarify his use of the words "permanent mother substitute" by adding: "one person who steadily mothers him". Nowhere did he clarify his use of the word "continuous", and this was to get him into a great deal of trouble later on. It is worth noting here that if you look up the word "attachment" in the index of *Child Care and the Growth of Love,* you will not find it. He had not worked it out in 1952, and did not use it in a publication until 1957.

Video clip of John Bowlby

> What I noticed was that there were children who had been referred for persistent thieving, truancy, and what I spotted was that they had had very, very disrupted childhoods. A continuous relationship between a mother and child in which both find happiness and satisfaction, promotes mental health.

Notice again his use of the word "continuous"; he frequently used it but did not distinguish between what he meant by "the enduring relationship" from that of "unbroken contact".

Child Care and the Growth of Love was primarily addressing children's experience of complete maternal deprivation, or prolonged separation, when abandoned in orphanages; he saw this as being "foremost among the causes of delinquent character development". He clarified the term "prolonged separation" as being "complete and prolonged separation, six months or more, from their mothers or established foster-mothers." However, the phrase "prolonged separation" has been misrepresented and frequently used to suggest that Attachment Theory warns of grave consequences for the young child whose mother works outside the home. For example, in 1998, in her best-seller *Life after Birth*—which is about working mothers—Kate Figes adds a distorting twist to a passage from my father's paperback; she says:

> He advises that mother should not work outside the home and warns that there is a very strong case indeed for believing that prolonged separation of a child from its mother or mother substitute during the first five years of life stands foremost among the causes of delinquent character development.

Figes equates the effect of mothers working outside the home for some hours a day with the effects of prolonged separation of six months or more, or even death. It is partly such confusion in popular books that has made Attachment Theory look so ridiculous that people dismiss it, along with Bowlby, out of hand.

In 1958, five years after *Child Care and the Growth of Love* was published, my father wrote a pamphlet called *Can I Leave my Baby?* I think he wrote this to clarify his position and to answer some of his critics, but the damage had already been done in the widely-read paperback and his pamphlet was only a minor publication:

> Mothers sometimes ask: "Then can we never leave our small children?" I do not believe that anyone has ever suggested they should not. It is an excellent plan to accustom babies and small children to being cared for, now and then, by someone else—father, for instance, or Granny, or some other relation or neighbour; in this way mother can have some freedom too, for an afternoon's shopping in peace, visits to the doctor or dentist, the cinema or tea with friends.

> Leaving small children whilst you go out to work needs much more care. If your own mother is living nearby or a dependable

neighbour can be daily guardian, it may work out all right. But it needs regularity, and it must be the same woman who cares for him.

It is the same with nannies. Nannies are valuable people, provided they are good ones and provided they stay. It is the chopping and changing of people in charge of a young child which upsets him. If a mother hands over her baby completely to a nanny (as my father was) she should realise that in her child's eyes, Nanny will be the real mother figure, not Mummy. This may be no bad thing, always provided that the care is continuous, but for a child to be looked after entirely by a loving nanny and then for her to leave when he is two or three, or even four or five, can be almost as tragic as the loss of a mother.

That's straight autobiography! I do not think he realized it was the word "continuous" that was the cause of the misunderstanding in the first place. I think his own loss of Minnie must have created a complete blind spot for him; otherwise, considering that the prime purpose of his pamphlet was to clarify what he meant by "continuous care", he would surely have defined the word "continuous". I suspect he was so deeply affected by this experience of a discontinued relationship that, to him, the meaning of a continuous relationship was so blindingly obvious and of such overpowering significance that it never even occurred to him that it might need defining. I would define his use of "continuous" (when applied to a relationship) as an enduring relationship, lasting many years, where periods of separation are shorter than would cause the child distress or trauma. The length of the period will depend upon the age of the child, the person with whom they are left, where they are left, how often they are left, and also the child's temperament and the quality of his relationship with their principal attachment figure—that is, the person who is leaving him.

The following video clip of my father is a bit confusing because he makes a Freudian slip, an example of a lack of coherent narrative: he refers to his mother as his grandmother.

Video clip of John Bowlby interview

Interviewer: "Do you think a nanny intervenes in the relationship between a mother and her child?"

John Bowlby: "Not necessarily; only if one is jealous of the other
    ... but if each have their own role and the parents
    see plenty of the children, there is no problem. I think
    one of the problems nowadays is that nannies don't
    stay. I mean, in my day I had a nanny. I was one of
    six children. Nanny came when my elder sister was a
    baby and stayed until my grandmother died at the
    age of ninety. She was part of the family, you see.
    That was a way of life which has long since ceased;
    I happened to notice just the other day that the Prin-
    cess of Wales' nanny had left after she was with the
    family for four years; she has now left and that, I am
    sure, is very unsettling for the two princes. Nannies
    leaving can be very traumatic, especially if the chil-
    dren have become very attached to them."

Interviewer: "So time is the important thing rather than . . .?"

John Bowlby: "Continuity is one very important thing, and the
    personal relationship between nanny and mother is
    the other critical thing. If they each have their own
    role it's all right; if they compete, it's all wrong."

A fundamental principle of Attachment Theory is that people of all
ages show a preference for one primary attachment figure above all
others; this will usually shift from the primary attachment figure,
usually the birth mother but not necessarily, to a romantic partner
over time. For babies older than a few months, the primary attachment figure is almost always the biological mother but it could be
anyone else who takes on the long-term commitment of raising the
child. My father told me how the arrangement of someone's attachment figures can be described as a pyramid: friends and familiar
neighbours at the base, secondary attachment figures above them,
and the primary attachment figure at the top. In *Attachment*
(Volume I) he comments that it may be confusing to refer to all of
them as "attachment figures", and to all the behaviour as "attachment behaviour". He was keen to emphasize that we need *multiple*
attachment figures, but that they are arranged in a hierarchy. In
Separation (Volume II) he says:

> Whether a child or adult is in a state of security, anxiety or distress
> is determined in large part by the accessibility and responsiveness
> of his principal attachment figure.

If a child has a surrogate carer, parents may fear that it will be the surrogate carer, not themselves, who will take that special top spot in the child's affections. It is of the greatest importance to the child that the initial primary attachment figure should be accessible for many years, preferably well into adulthood. I accept, of course, that there are many situations when the sensitive use of good quality, age-appropriate substitute care is the realistic choice for parents. Sarah Blaffer Hrdy, a Professor of Anthropology, in her excellent book *Mother Nature*, explains how she used her knowledge of Attachment Theory to arrange day care for her baby. The programme at the Harvard Yard Day Care Centre, which she used, was designed by Berry Brazelton, a leading advocate of Attachment Theory; Professor Hrdy describes a facility that worked so well precisely because it addressed the various attachment needs of the children.

In 1951 my father met Konrad Lorenz; it was a red-letter day for him. He had read Lorenz's work on the imprinting of goslings and how they incessantly followed the first moving object they saw during the crucial early phase. This was an inspiration to my father and he began to examine the biological origins of an infant's "proximity-seeking" behaviour. Imprinting is a bit different to attachment, for the birds evolve from a different stem, but nevertheless the behaviour was sufficiently close to arouse his interest. Birds had always been a source of fascination to him—in fact, I got involved in photography because I discovered the camera that he had used as a naval cadet at Dartmouth College to indulge his hobby of photographing nesting birds.

Being on sabbatical in Palo Alto in 1957 gave my father enough time to pull together all the strands of his work. This was when he said to me:

> You know this business about the instinct for a small child to stay
> close to its mother, and the intimate relationship they form, well,
> I believe that it's the same instinct to form close relationships that
> stays with us all our lives; and we suffer the same feelings of loss
> when a loved one dies as a child feels who's lost his mother.

The following year he read a paper to the British Psycho-Analytic Society (BPAS) called *The Nature of the Child's Tie to its Mother*, in which he first outlined what was to become known as Attachment Theory. This paper was received with great hostility in London; an orchestrated attack on his ideas was mounted. I believe that it was on this occasion that somebody remarked "Very interesting, Dr Bowlby, but what has it got to do with psychoanalysis?" He considered this paper was a watershed in his career—because it simultaneously outlined the basis of the attachment relationship, and also alienated him from the vast majority of his professional psychoanalytic peers for many years to come. Not only was he challenging many of the theories of Klein and Freud, but he was presenting a coherent alternative theory instead. To psychoanalysts at the time, many with unbearable traumas in their past, this new theory must have been deeply disturbing. Years later, in 1987, he remarked: "I have found it extremely unfashionable to attribute psychopathology to real-life experiences."

It is important to realize how many years it took my father to work all this out, and what a struggle it was to establish which parts of the jigsaw fitted where; which bits belonged to a different puzzle; and which bits were just rubbish. Many people still think that he created Attachment Theory fully-formed, in an instant of time, in 1950. He did not. People say he changed his mind; well, the seeds were sown when he was four years old; he was forty-six when *Child Care and the Growth of Love* came out; and he was seventy-three when he completed the Attachment trilogy. I think it is reasonable to assume that there was some development in his knowledge between the ages of four and seventy-three. As for changes of mind, Germaine Greer writes in *The Whole Woman*, (published 2002):

> In *The Female Eunuch* I argued that motherhood should not be treated as a substitute career; now I would argue that motherhood should be regarded as a genuine career option, that is to say, as paid work and, as such, as an alternative to other paid work. What this would mean is that every woman who decides to have a child would be paid enough money to raise that child in decent circumstances.

My father supported the view, in print, that mothers should receive proper financial support from the State for the first three years of their child's life.

His guiding principle was that: "If the theory doesn't fit the data, change the theory, not the data." It took him years to develop a theory of attachment that incorporated all the research data that his colleagues had amassed; only then did he start to write the three volumes. I think his forthright manner made him the champion of those who felt supported by him, but a pariah to those who felt threatened by his ideas; I fear there has been a limited meeting of minds as a result.

Video clip of John Bowlby interview

John Bowlby: "About sixty per cent of mothers do a very good job, so the majority of women have a good model to follow—and there is an awful lot to be said for that."

Interviewer: "So you are saying that 40 per cent do not do a good job?"

John Bowlby: "I am."

Interviewer: "And what does that mean?"

John Bowlby: "Well, it means a lot of mental ill-health and disturbance and delinquency and what have you."

Well, that's telling you! No wonder he had his battles! In taking up this principle, I try to be as thoughtful and as considerate as I can, but I do think that these issues have to be addressed. One cannot just sweep great chunks of human nature under the carpet; these are the chunks that make us who we are, that make us human. He considered the best conditions for optimum mental health for children under three years old were:

> a resourceful parent (usually but not necessarily, the biological mother) who was happy to stay at home, with adequate emotional, practical and financial support, where both the parent and child found satisfaction and enjoyment.

My wife, Xenia, was a full-time, stay-at-home mother; she is sometimes asked what it was like to live next door to John Bowlby and bring up his grandchildren. She says that he only ever once gave her advice. This was in 1968, when she was pregnant for the second time and under some peer pressure to stop providing "'comfort on demand" for our two-year-old. (They said: "You'll make a rod for your own back.") He said to her: "Carry on exactly as you are; take no notice of what others say, you are doing it right." I think that may be a message for some of us to take away tonight. Our daughter Sophie and her husband Matt have recently had a baby and bought a small house. They told us that when house-hunting, they had drawn a three-mile circle around our house, and had only looked at places inside that circle.

I now turn to some of the financial and emotional obstacles that have made Attachment Theory so unpalatable to the public. Humans have an insatiable appetite for knowledge and invention aimed at making life better and easier. However, our genetically inherited developmental needs remain unchanged. If we allow them to be submerged by the lifestyle that technological and social progress has made available, we get into trouble. I was born in 1941 and people of my age are now becoming grandparents; we can see some of our children struggling to arrange their lives and afford the lifestyle that they have grown to accept—the lifestyle and values adopted by my generation. We need to look at the care of small children from the perspective of their parents, the thirty-something generation of new mothers and fathers.

Two big changes during my lifetime can be singled out. First is the dramatic increase in wealth and living standards that much of society enjoys, compared with the 1940s and 1950s when I was a child in England. The second change is perhaps even more dramatic: the huge social and cultural changes brought about by the equal opportunities movement in the 1970s. This opened up to a much wider spectrum of society an array of social, educational, and employment possibilities that had previously been closed on grounds of race, gender, age, class, or creed. The consequent rise in living standards and disposable income for a broad band of middle-class young people raised their expectations very high. These included good housing, transport, holidays, television, designer clothes, mobile phones, central heating, entertainment and leisure activities—not to mention PCs, CDs, plasma screens and all those gizmos. These expectations have been created by my generation and it is not unreasonable for my children to wish to provide these high standards for their own families. However, they need to pay for this lifestyle and, particularly nowadays, decent housing is expensive. As a result, many new families feel they have little or no choice but to continue earning two salaries throughout their child-rearing years. Having choices is very important and these financial pressures drastically limit the choice of most parents.

I want to touch on the emotional sensitivity of new parents, and in particular the reaction that information on attachment findings produces when people first encounter it. Let me first, however, acknowledge that some parents of small babies feel that parenting would be so frustrating to them that the baby would fare better with long periods of day care and shorter periods of their own "quality time". It must also be acknowledged that in some very dysfunctional circumstances, long periods of non-parental care, foster-care or even adoption may be needed to reduce the trans-mission of dysfunction to the baby. Lastly, I respect anybody who does not have children at all.

Most informal discussions with parents about attachment-related issues rapidly become focused on their own personal expe-riences. These reflections may go back to childhood memories of family pleasures, or the pain of family breakdown, or of personal trauma; sometimes people also worry about the parenting arrange-ments for their own children. The problem here is that much of the memory of childhood is, as this audience will certainly know, stored at the unconscious level. Triggering these memories makes some parents very uncomfortable although they are not sure why; fight, flight, or freeze may be the instinctive response that emerges.

Of the many difficulties surrounding parenting issues, I think day care is the most contentious. One outspoken psychologist, Jay Belsky, has created controversy by spreading the findings of the massive National Institute of Child Health and Development (NICHD) study of day care for over 1,200 children. In spring 2001 the results were released for the cohort which had reached the age of four-and-a-half years. Belsky was quoted as saying:

> We find clearly, indisputably and unambiguously that the more time spent in care, the more likely [the children] are to be aggres-sive and disobedient. . . . Even more surprising, the results are the same regardless of the type of quality of day care, the sex of the child, or whether the family is rich or poor. What seems to matter

most is time. The more hours spent away from parents, the more likely is the child to have behavioural problems. . . . In no case can the findings be described as strong, but a small impact on many may be of far greater social significance than a large impact on a few.

Many parents who have no choice but to work will find these words painful, and will not want to hear them. I think there is a similarity between the way my father was treated when he delivered his uncomfortable message many years ago and the way Belsky is being treated today when he reports the more uncomfortable aspects of the NICHD day care study. I did, by the way, take this quote to Belsky to check he was comfortable with my using the piece; he confirmed that it was accurate and that he would stand by it. When I likened the struggle that he was having to my father's struggle, he said: "I think it has something to do with the initials!"

There is currently a culture glorifying the independence of the nuclear family who can make it on their own without being dependent on anyone else, and of denigrating the inter-dependence of the extended family. Peer pressure often encourages mothers to return to work promptly, aided by attractive employment offers which may not be available after a maternity break of several years. Many young couples have made financial commitments which require them both to return to work after the birth of a baby; there is often, however, a dramatic shift in their feelings once the new baby arrives, and they may come to regret entering into those commitments. There are some positive reports about the advantages of modern childcare arrangements that are reassuring to new parents:

- Playing with other infants in day care helps the social development of the child.
- Infants have a better standard of living with two-income parents.
- Day care infants have a larger vocabulary and are more ready for pre-school facilities.
- Working parents are less depressed and isolated than stay-at-home parents.
- High-quality day care can compensate for a very poor family environment.

- Childcare professionals are more experienced and know how to stimulate babies.

There are also reports of problems associated with modern day care arrangements:

- Parents are less sensitive to the baby's cues for attention if they are apart all day.
- Only one in ten day care places is rated as high-quality, and for many these are unaffordable or unavailable.
- The more time an infant under three is apart from his parents, the more likely he is to be aggressive.
- When multiple care-workers look after a baby, there is a negative impact on his emotional development.
- Separating a small child from a surrogate primary attachment figure can leave lasting emotional scars.

In 1987, on my father's eightieth birthday, the *Boston Globe* quoted from an interview with him where he had said: "What astonishes me most about family life in the United States is that mothers tell me they can't afford to look after their own babies—in the richest country in the world!" He felt that society had overlooked the enormous amount of time involved in delivering emotionally enriching parenting, and that we too often short-change our infants. He thought that making appropriate arrangements for the care of babies and small children needed the intelligent application of Attachment Theory in order to avoid the pitfalls of the past. I realize that there is no benefit in ramming Attachment Theory down the throats of vulnerable parents who cannot alter their circumstances. We need, therefore, to find new ways of opening up the debate before people become locked into decisions they later regret.

How to be a good enough parent, or whether our own parents were good enough for us, or if our children will become good enough parents, or even the definition of a good enough parent, are powerful attachment issues that most people find difficult to talk about. It is frightening to enter the world of scientifically demonstrable evidence concerning the long-term mental health of children. The irony is that it is often people's own past attachment experiences that prevent them from having a clearer understanding of Attachment Theory.

Video clip of John Bowlby

I think boys learn an enormous amount from being apprenticed to their fathers and girls learn an enormous amount by being apprenticed to their mothers. This is the usual pattern. It's not necessary, but it is the common pattern. Children flourish on attention from adults and if children get an adult's attention, and affection, and enjoyment, and company, and so on, they prosper. So many children unfortunately don't get that from their parents and grandparents. I would say you cannot over-estimate the importance of parental attitudes towards children. It is absolutely crucial. The lessons here are frightfully simple and people who neglect their children do not like hearing them; that's the trouble!

Did you notice that he was quite emotionally choked at one point? It was obviously a very personal message that he brought, but he always tried just to stick with the data. He was guided by his feelings, by his experiences, but he used classic scientific methods in his work and stuck very carefully to the science. His article "Psychoanalysis as Art and Science", is a particularly helpful way of looking at these matters.

An article written shortly after the death of my father summed up, in a sentence, the dilemma between parents' social aspirations and the demands on them as parents. That sentence, which I quote from memory, was: "Why couldn't John Bowlby come up with a theory of child development that was more appropriate [sic] to the needs of modern parents?" The dilemma is plain to see in such distorted logic. Part of the trouble is the word "theory"—I've got my theory, you've got yours, and we can have any old theory! Our use of the word "theory" in common parlance is very loose, so why shouldn't somebody come up with a theory that suits us better if you are not using the word in the proper, strictest scientific sense? It is a bad word. I use it here because you all understand what I mean, but I don't use it to a general public audience.

Over the years there has been a polarizing of opinion, whipped up by the media, between those who are vehemently against attachment thinking as they understand it, and those who are passionately in favour of their version of it. This destructive polarization of opinion prevents the general public from getting a balanced view of Attachment Theory. Let me summarize the four main factors that I believe are preventing the knowledge of Attachment Theory from becoming more widely accepted by the general public:

1.   Some people are securely attached and are comfortable with their life choices, hence the topic is of little concern to them.
2.   Some are confused by the widespread misrepresentation and ridicule of my father's work in the popular media.
3.   Some have personal memories of painful childhood issues that are awakened by the insights afforded by Attachment Theory.
4.   Some are anxious about the long-term consequences that limited parenting choices may have for their own children.

The research data on many aspects of Attachment Theory is now unassailable. Somebody recently asked me if I had attended a "big conference in Minneapolis". I had not, and asked why I should have gone there. The answer was: "It was astonishing; there were 3,500 people and the only show in town was your father's work!" Despite that, the way we have been communicating this knowledge to the general public for the past fifty years has not been effective. Many lay people are still mystified by the emotional and social development of their children. For me, the challenge ahead is to find new and appropriate ways to help ordinary men and women to benefit from my father's knowledge.

Vote of thanks by Brett Kahr

Thank you very much, Sir Richard. I think we all realize how lucky we are—those of us who practise in the fields of psychology, counselling, psychoanalysis, or psychotherapy—that Sir Richard has now retired from his post at the Royal Free Hospital, and therefore may devote himself full-time to the furtherance of his research. He has actually given a great gift to those of us who work as mental health professionals.

Introduction of Pearl King

Brett Kahr

We have a further treat tonight. Pearl King has kindly
accepted our invitation to follow Sir Richard Bowlby this
evening, and to share with us her personal and unique
reminiscences of both Donald Winnicott, the man, and John Bowlby,
the man. Pearl is one of the few people alive today who worked very
closely with both, and who knew each of them in a variety of
contexts. It is vitally important for those of us who are students,
entering the psychoanalytical or psychotherapeutic field for the first
time, confronted by an often confusing and overwhelming array of
historical personalities, to begin to learn about competing theories
by first understanding the man or the woman behind these theories.
In this spirit, we have called upon Pearl King to provide us with
some biographical meat and potatoes, if you will, something to
underpin our knowledge of these two towering figures in the
burgeoning disciplines of infant and child mental health.

Pearl King occupies a unique position in the international
psychoanalytical movement. She has practised as a psychoanalyst for over fifty years, having become the very first non-
medical President of the British Psycho-Analytical Society, and
having served as Secretary to the International Psycho-Analytical

Association as well. She recently received the Sigourney Award, the highest honour that one can earn in the field of psychoanalysis, arguably the psychoanalytical equivalent of an Academy Award or the BAFTA, for lifetime achievement. Not only a psychoanalyst of great clinical renown—one of the most popular teachers, supervisors, and mentors—within the British mental health community, she will also be well-known to us as an exceptional historian of psychoanalysis, and as the founder of the Archives of the British Psycho-Analytical Society, recently renamed as The Pearl King Archives Trust in commemoration of the important work that she has done to keep the history of psychoanalysis alive. Her wonderful book, co-authored with Professor Riccardo Steiner, *The Freud–Klein Controversies: 1941–45* (King & Steiner, 1991), remains a work of exceptional scholarship, translated into many languages around the world. Only a short while ago, Miss King received the very exciting news that a Chinese translation would be appearing in print before too long. This will be followed by an edition of her collected papers, currently in preparation, which will be published by Karnac Books.

During a recent research trip to New York City, I found another interesting letter. Pearl herself may not have seen this letter since 1961. It is a letter that Donald Winnicott wrote to Pearl King about John Bowlby. At that time, Pearl served as the Chairman of the Publications Committee of the Institute of Psycho-Analysis, and in this capacity wrote to Dr Winnicott asking what he would think about including a book by John Bowlby in the International Psycho-Analytical Library. Winnicott (1961) wrote:

> From several quarters I have heard that Dr. Bowlby might be offering a book to the Library for publication. Any book by Bowlby would be a profitable book to publish and would be read all over the world in places where psycho-analysis is scarcely read at all. Nevertheless I think that it is unlikely that one of Bowlby's books, of which he has given us samples, would qualify for publication in the International Library, and I doubt whether the Society would be satisfied if it were found that Dr Bowlby's offer of a book had been accepted.

In this respect, Winnicott alluded to the tension felt by many psychoanalysts at that time, who believed that Bowlby had abandoned the principles of orthodox psychoanalysis (cf. Grosskurth, 1986). This excerpt provides a marvellous summation of the points made by Sir Richard Bowlby in his lecture, namely, that although Bowlby has received deep appreciation internationally, many of his colleagues closer to home have not always understood his work—colleagues in many cases now long since deceased, and remembered by few.

Pearl King has always remained a modern psychoanalyst in the best sense of the word. She recognized the brilliance of both Bowlby and Winnicott, and encouraged their work. In a further letter, written by Pearl King (1962) to Donald Winnicott, she urged: "I hope that you are yourself seriously considering writing a book to be included in this Library. It does not have to be very long, if you are pressed for time." Fortunately for us all, Winnicott obliged, and in 1965, the International Psycho-Analytical Library published one of the great masterpieces of Winnicott's (1965) oeuvre, *The Maturational Processes and the Facilitating Environment: Studies in the Theory of Emotional Development*.

It is my very great privilege to invite Pearl King to offer her reflections and her reminiscences about these two extraordinary psychoanalytical pioneers. Ladies and gentlemen, please welcome Pearl King.

References

Grosskurth, P. (1986). *Melanie Klein: Her World and Her Work*. New York: Alfred A. Knopf.

King, P. (1962). Letter to Donald W. Winnicott. 17th May. Box 3. File 3. Archives of Psychiatry. The Oskar Diethelm Library. Institute for the History of Psychiatry. Department of Psychiatry. Joan and Sanford I. Weill Medical College. Cornell University. The New York Presbyterian Hospital, New York, USA.

King, P., & Steiner, R. (Eds.). (1991). *The Freud–Klein Controversies: 1941–45*. London: Tavistock/Routledge.

Winnicott, D. W. (1961). Letter to Pearl King. 18th July. Box 3. File 3. Archives of Psychiatry. The Oskar Diethelm Library. Institute for the History of Psychiatry. Department of Psychiatry. Joan and Sanford I. Weill Medical College. Cornell University. The New York Presbyterian Hospital, New York, USA.

Winnicott, D. W. (1965). *The Maturational Processes and the Facilitating Environment: Studies in the Theory of Emotional Development.* London: Hogarth Press and the Institute of Psycho-Analysis.

Recollections of Donald Winnicott and John Bowlby

Pearl King

I could not help thinking, while I was listening to Sir Richard, how a cousin of mine who was a medical missionary in India once said to me: "This Dr Bowlby, you know, I think that the devil must have got into him!" It was enough to make one feel very worried and wonder what else this man would come up with. You see, my cousin had gone to India as a medical missionary, leaving two of her children, one of whom was a "blue" baby, at home to be looked after by relatives.

At that time many more people worked abroad in the mission-field where it was not very easy to keep their children with them. Their usual response to their dilemma was: "God called me to go abroad; I am doing His will; He will look after the children!"

I have some personal experience in this context, for I "lost" my mother, and my father, so to speak, when I was four years old. My parents were Christian missionaries and they went abroad to East Africa, taking my new baby brother with them and leaving me behind with a family of four cousins, two older and two younger than me. I lived with them for four years and they became my "family". When I was eight years old, my parents returned from abroad and I "lost" my family; in return, I was left with a sad little

31

boy who did not know how to play and often cried. After a year, my parents returned to Africa and I was sent, together with my five-year-old brother, to a boarding-school.

I was most upset about losing the family of cousins who had become my "family". This boarding-school accepted only children of active CMS missionaries, so that we all shared a common "trauma", i.e., that of separation from parents for years, with no family life in the holidays. After a year or two at the school, feeling rather dumped and unwanted, some of us decided to organize ourselves into groups, in which we were protected from the bullying tactics of unhappy classmates.

It is now interesting to me to see how a group of children, treated in this way, worked out together a way of making up for the loss, or temporary absence, of their real family. There is no doubt that we formed ourselves into "extended families". The lesson that I draw from this experience is that even though many colleagues (including John Bowlby) would regard the situation in which we grew up as potentially traumatic, it turned out better than might be expected, because those involved took the trouble to "work out" how best to cope in that situation. True, we were "merely" children, but we had the capability of realizing that we needed extended and continuing relationships and we created them for ourselves. Anyone who knows anything about my professional activities would recognize that I have been forming "groups" to protect people, or promote ideas, ever since!

Today I am here to talk about Donald Winnicott and John Bowlby. They were both very good friends of mine. I worked with both of them in the British Psycho-Analytical Society (BPAS) and I accomplished much good work with each of them. Following a period of "unrest" and "problems" in the Society, in 1956 John was elected Deputy President and I was elected as Honorary Business Secretary. John was very convinced about the importance of an institution having an appropriate structure and together we managed to introduce some new procedures into the Society and to put in place a structure that would give protection to its members.

In preparation for this evening, I consulted records, including Minutes of the Society and its Annual Reports, to see what Donald was doing at this time when John was Deputy President. To my surprise, I saw that Donald was then the President of the Society. It seemed very odd that I should have forgotten that, until I remembered that Donald Winnicott, on the whole, did not like committee meetings and that is probably why we had comparatively little contact. Although he was a member of the Council, he did not have to attend its meetings. He chaired the Scientific Meetings and left John and me to carry on the business of the Society.

After a year working together, John Bowlby was invited to spend a year at Palo Alto, in the States, doing research and writing. William Gillespie, another person who cared deeply about people and the importance of good organization, was elected, at the AGM in July 1957, as Deputy President—and therefore as Chairman of the Board and Council—with myself as Business Secretary again. What I had not bargained for was that at the Paris Congress of the International Psycho-Analytical Association (IPA) in 1957 he was to be elected as President of that organization and that he would choose me as its Honorary Secretary!

While John was abroad, he began putting psychoanalytic theory through a very tough questioning, with the aim of seeing how theory could help with what he had been discovering in his work with children and with the ideas he was beginning to conceptualize. When he returned to the UK in 1958 he began writing all those papers that were to cause him so many problems with his professional peers. Over the next few years he read a number of his papers to the Scientific Meetings of the Society. One paper was discussed at three successive meetings; another occupied two consecutive meetings. Sadly, at that time we did not record our scientific discussions; although we know who spoke at the meetings, we have no written record of what was said. If they had been recorded, people's reactions to John's controversial papers would now make interesting reading. It was a very anxious time for the Society, especially for those members who had their own particular point of view and expected other people to follow it.

To return to the time when John returned from Palo Alto in 1958, he was again elected as Deputy President, a position which he held for another three years. He continued to serve the Society in that role, while I withdrew from the Council to work as Honorary Secretary of the IPA with William Gillespie. Once I was no longer a member of the Society's Board and Council, my only contact with

John for the next three years was when I attended his research discussion groups on the effects of separation on children.

On the occasion of John's eightieth birthday, I insisted on reading a paper about his contributions to the Society and Institute (King, 1987). I decided that although many colleagues had not been able to appreciate him earlier, at least they would now have to spend a whole hour listening to me describing all the things he had done for us. He was present for this meeting, and indeed the whole family was there. The fact that this event took place was a little unusual. I like to think that it was an attempt to say sorry to him for the unkind way he had been treated by some members of the Society.

When John died, Eric Rayner and I wrote his obituary (King & Rayner 1993) and insisted that it was published in the *International Journal of Psycho-Analysis*; it ran to six pages. We felt that all members of the IPA who read that journal should be made aware of his achievements—and that those who had been unable to reach some kind of accommodation with his ideas could have another chance to do so. To us, it was curious that John's work and thinking was known all over both Americas and elsewhere, and that people outside the UK seemed to know better than most of our members how useful his contributions had been and what research they had inspired.

I first got to know Donald Winnicott quite well in 1951, after I had qualified. I asked him to supervise a child case for me. He selected a severely traumatized four-year-old boy, who tried to beat me up from time to time. However, in the end that child did very well and I learned so much from Donald. Not only did I get to know him, but I started to understand his way of thinking about problems and psychoanalysis. At one time when I was treating this child, I became quite frightened of the boy, who was really quite strong! What helped me to deal with my fears was Winnicott's comment to me: "You'll be all right, Pearl," he said, "provided he doesn't think he is God. When a child thinks he's God, he never misses!"

It was some years later when we again worked together, this time as members of the BPAS Council. For a period of twelve years either John Bowlby, Donald Winnicott or I were on the Council of the BPAS. At one period when I was Deputy President and Winnicott was President, we discussed beforehand what matters to bring up at Council. At that time, I lived in Great Cumberland

Place, Marble Arch, which he passed on his way to his home near Victoria. Sometimes he would give me a lift to my flat. I recall that after one Council meeting when I had been chatting, as one does, about a topic which interested me, he offered me a lift home. When we were in the car, quite suddenly, out of the blue, he said: "If only Melanie Klein had once, just once, said to me that she had learned something from Donald Winnicott, I would be satisfied." I replied: "How very sad for her, because she cut herself off from so much learning that she could have enjoyed."

It was indeed sad to realize that in the BPAS at that time we had Anna Freud, who had expert knowledge of children in the latency period; Melanie Klein, who had set her sights on very young children, trying to analyse them and so had a lot to give; Winnicott, who had so much experience to share, gained from his clinic; and then there was John, who had also gained much experience in Child Guidance Clinics and his research on mother–child relationships. They were all giants in their own particular way. Yet they seemed so often to be either at odds with each other, or indifferent to each other's work. They never seemed to share experiences or exchange information.

I am now in my eighty-fifth year, and looking back on fifty years of working with these exceptionally gifted people, I think about what could have happened had there been more co-operation, or even just friendliness, between them all. I am sure that it would have been tremendous and so beneficial for everyone in the Society, especially for those working with children.

Winnicott had great difficulty in persuading any of his colleagues to let him come into contact with the teaching side of the Institute of Psycho-Analysis. He was allowed three evenings a year. He complained to Sylvia Payne, and later to Adam Limentani, because he could not build up a relationship with students when he only had three seminars a year in which to do so.

I wonder what his colleagues were afraid of? Could it be that they were afraid their own students would pick up Winnicott's way of letting himself *think* about what was being said at Scientific Meetings, instead of just checking to see whether or not a speaker followed their party line? Alongside criticizing those who contributed to discussions, Winnicott encouraged colleagues to think for themselves; he urged that when they reported their work, they should do more than simply copy the ideas of their own training analyst. In 1954 he wrote to Roger Money-Kyrle as follows:

> I found myself getting annoyed talking to you last night. I did not want to leave it like that as I have a great respect for you, and not a little affection. I think what irritated me was that I faintly detected in your attitude this matter of a party line, a matter to which I am allergic. Your *own* opinion is what I asked for. . . . When people like Marion Milner, or myself for that matter, write papers, we do not write them in order to show each time that we have grasped Melanie Klein's contributions to theory, but we write them because of an original idea that needs ventilating.'[Rodman, 1987]

The message that Winnicott seems to be trying to convey to adherents and their students, if only they would learn it from him, was how much more pleasure they could experience if they dared to have a more open mind by allowing themselves to see the whole context in which their patients struggled, which included external settings and relationships as well as their inner world. I suspect that John's interest in the external relationships was something that did not win him friends in the Society; people used to tut-tut about him, saying he did not place enough emphasis on "the inner world".

Winnicott seemed happier with his colleagues when he was President of the Society. He was elected after the Freud Centenary in 1956 and held office until 1959. During the time I worked with him, while Secretary to the BPAS, he was deeply concerned about raising money for a new child clinic, following the gift of $1,000 from Pryns Hopkins, who had helped Ernest Jones to start the adult clinic in 1926. The child clinic was opened in 1960.

Winnicott understood the importance of parties for his colleagues, in contrast with the rather precious attitudes of some of them. I remember particularly his pleasure in the party he helped to arrange for Melanie Klein's seventy-fifth birthday. This was followed by a party for Joan Riviere's seventieth birthday in 1958— which was more tricky to organize because Joan Riviere did not want to invite Melanie Klein to it. I think Paula Heimann helped to sort the situation out and Mrs Klein came to it for a short time. In 1966 Winnicott had his seventieth birthday. He and Clare put on the best party at Mansfield House that I have ever attended. We ate and danced, then sat on the floor and listened to Joan Baez singing.

Winnicott also successfully campaigned for funds to commemorate Freud with a statue of himself by Oscar Nemon, cast in bronze and erected outside Swiss Cottage Library. He and Anna Freud unveiled this in October 1970. The statue has now been moved to stand outside the Tavistock Clinic in Belsize Lane.

Another period when Donald and I worked particularly closely together was when he was appointed Chairman of the Sponsoring Committee of the Finnish Psychoanalytical Society and I was appointed Honorary Secretary to the Committee. The task of the Sponsoring Committee was to set up interim training arrangements for the Finnish candidates so that they could train as psychoanalysts during the period until the Study Group became a Component Society of the International Psychoanalytical Association. This training role, perhaps, made up a little for Donald having been excluded from participating in the training activities of the British Society; I hope so.

While he was working with our Finnish colleagues, Winnicott announced that he was going to present a case that had not gone very well. He explained to me that he did this so that the students could feel that they, too, could make mistakes; he wanted them to understand that this would not matter, provided they were firmly rooted in the *spirit* of the psychoanalytic tradition, rather than just following the letter of it. I saw this as his independent mind at work (King, 2000). Most people in his position would want to show how clever they were! One very important thing that I learned from working with Winnicott on this project was how important it was to leave enough space around individuals who were learning, for them to be able to think for themselves, and for them in turn to learn to leave enough space around their patients for them—so that both could discover their own unique way of thinking and working creatively.

References

King, P. (1987). John Bowlby's contributions to the British Psychoanalytical Society and its organisation. *Scientific Bulletin of the British*

Psycho-Analytical Society, September (also published in the *Scientific Bulletin of the British Psycho-Analytical Society*, November 1991, together with other contributions given at his Memorial Meeting, 16 October , 1991).

King, P., & Rayner, E. (1993). Obituary—John Bowlby (1907–1990). *International Journal of Psycho-Analysis, 74*: 823–828.

King, P. (2000). Winnicott as an independent mind. Paper read to the Winnicott Congress in Milan, November 2000 (to be included in a book of Congress papers).

Rodman, F. R. (Ed.) (1987). *The Spontaneous Gesture—Selected Letters of D. W. Winnicott*, pp. 79–80. Cambridge, MA: Harvard University Press.

Vote of thanks by Brett Kahr

Thank you so much, Pearl, for your beautiful historical impressions. You have succeeded in bringing both John Bowlby and Donald Winnicott back to life in a most splendid manner. We eagerly await the publication of your collected papers, and we thank you for joining us here this evening. Fortunately, we now have an opportunity for questions and comments from colleagues in the audience.

Questions to Sir Richard Bowlby

Group 1

Why is it that the work and ideas of Dr Bowlby are so much more widely known and practised in the United States than here? Is this simply a cultural matter, or is it because American society is, on the whole, very much more orientated towards psychoanalytic theories generally? Are Americans much quicker than us to accept new ideas? Is there any specific reason, for example, that childcare arrangements for my daughter-in-law, who is resident in America, are very much based on Attachment Theory?

1. *The reason my father's work and ideas are so much wider-known and practised in the United States than in the United Kingdom—so much so that many child care arrangements are very closely based on his Attachment Theory—is probably a cultural phenomenon. Americans are more orientated towards psychoanalytic theories generally, and their way of thinking is more attuned to taking on new ideas. I recall an American saying to me (and this is not at all PC): "Don't forget, Richard, nearly every American has come from a disrupted background—and those who*

did have stable backgrounds, we disrupted!" There is a resonance to my father's work which strikes a chord in America; it is a combination of the brave new world and the taking-on of new ideas in a positive way. Certainly Mary Ainsworth, who was in many ways a co-founder of Attachment Theory, is very highly regarded in America and has received the most prestigious awards.

Group 2

Has any theory been developed, or is any relevant work being done, on the split family? Although a growing number of families nowadays are being divided through one of the parents leaving, why is it that there is comparatively little information as to the most likely effects on the children who have suffered this attachment split? When there were split-ups involving children in my own family, I did not know how best to help the children; what is the most useful way for other family members to react to these sad circumstances? How does a child cope when the family is disintegrating and the day-to-day carers are no longer around all the time?

2. In a number of families nowadays one parent has quit the home, leaving a divided family—often one where the former day-to-day carer is no longer around all the time, or as much as was once the case. Children often bear the brunt of family disintegration and suffer greatly from the split with their attachment figures. Work is being done in this field, but it is an extremely delicate and sensitive area, not one in which I have been directly involved but I am naturally aware of the difficulties it presents to children. My father once said of this situation: "It may seem curious, but sometimes the outcome of a family break-up can be worse than the death of a parent." The death of a parent can be mourned; it is not an intended, deliberate act; it is a loss about which a child can openly grieve; there is a service and burial; there are rituals and traditions which comfort and console; there is support for the family.

Family breakdown is not like that; it is deliberate, and often occurs in most unpleasant circumstances. Generally, adults react by turning a blind eye to much of what is happening so far as any children are concerned, perhaps because we are not sure of how best to handle it. We defend ourselves, rather than biting the bullet and recognizing that the break-up will be very tough indeed for a child, because he will forever have as part of his past the knowledge that one of his parents walked out on him.

We raise defence mechanisms in order to ward off pain; that reaction is natural and very powerful; it helps us to cope; it can be too difficult, too painful, to consider the effects on the child; we avoid thinking about it very deeply. But defence mechanisms are blunt instruments. We can decide to chop out one element in our lives, but it not possible surgically to excise just that one piece; a lot of useful stuff goes as well. It is a problem, and a growing problem. It affects not just individual families but society as a whole. We all, not just the specialist groups here tonight, would benefit from greater insights into this painful area—and it is an area where I believe that Attachment Theory has much to offer by way of improving understanding of what is happening to children experiencing family break-down. We need to find ways to communicate better with the general public about bonding, and how children can be helped through this most difficult period.

Group 3

We who work in the counselling field are aware of the need for better guidance as we seek to help split families, which involve children; what, for example, are the in-depth, long-term effects of children losing their primary attachment figure? What are the implications of the current shortage of good childcare facilities? Do we know the long-term effects on children who enter the education system while still very young. Does losing carer continuity, for example when staff change, have a detrimental effect on children's development? What are the long-term effects of the current fashion in education of regular and frequent testing of children (which is a form of competition) right from a early age?

3. The Scandinavian system of day care for young children is rather like that which exists in many parts of America. Although young children go to school, they do not do what is generally considered in this country as "school-work". To a casual outside observer, it looks as if they are playing. In fact, certainly in Scandinavia, the teacher is facilitating the children's acquisition of interpersonal skills; they are learning to co-operate, to use adults when needed and to engage their co-operation to solve problems they cannot manage alone. Learning to be socially co-operative at a very young age is, I suspect, of more value than struggling—especially for dyslexics like me—to learn to read; that, after all, is a skill you can pick up very quickly when you are a bit older.

Envoi

Brett Kahr

Please join me in giving a warm vote of thanks to our two speakers this evening, Sir Richard Bowlby, and Miss Pearl King. We have had a marvellous fusion of the historical Winnicott and the historical Bowlby, with the contemporary applications of their evergreen contributions.

Eric Koops

I am indeed grateful to the speakers tonight. Each of us will take away our own memories of what has been said, and each of us will have gained a particular and personal insight into the various matters we have discussed. That, above all, is the value of gatherings such as this. We hope that we, in our small way, have done something useful in enabling this general sharing of experience in an interesting field, in bringing together people of like mind. Thank you all for coming.